SPORTS SUPERSTARS

WHO IS TRAVIS KELCE?

ZELDA WAGNER

Lerner Publications ◆ Minneapolis

Stats in this book are accurate through the 2024 National Football League season.

Lerner Publications Company
An imprint of Lerner Publishing Group, Inc.
241 First Avenue North
Minneapolis, MN 55401 USA

For reading levels and more information, look up this title at www.lernerbooks.com.

Main body text set in Mikado.
Typeface provided by HvD Fonts.

Designer: Mary Ross

Library of Congress Cataloging-in-Publication Data

Names: Wagner, Zelda, 2000- author
Title: Who is Travis Kelce? / Zelda Wagner.
Description: Minneapolis : Lerner Publications, [2026] | Series: Lerner Sports Rookie. Sports superstars | Stats in this book are accurate through the 2024 National Football League season. | Includes bibliographical references and index. | Audience: Ages 5–8 | Audience: Grades 2–3 | Summary: "Kansas City Chiefs tight end Travis Kelce has won three Super Bowls. His pass-catching ability is legendary. Explore his life and career"— Provided by publisher.
Identifiers: LCCN 2025026124 (print) | LCCN 2025026125 (ebook) | ISBN 9798765689646 lib. bdg. | ISBN 9798348029142 pbk | ISBN 9798765697986 epub
Subjects: LCSH: Kelce, Travis, 1989- | Kansas City Chiefs (Football team) | Tight ends (Football)—United States—Biography—Juvenile literature | Football players—United States—Biography—Juvenile literature | LCGFT: Statistics | Biographies
Classification: LCC GV939.K36 W34 2026 (print) | LCC GV939.K36 (ebook) | DDC 796.332092—dc23/eng/20250807

LC record available at https://lccn.loc.gov/2025026124
LC ebook record available at https://lccn.loc.gov/2025026125

Manufactured in the United States of America
1-1012765-54832-7/28/2025

TABLE OF CONTENTS

SUPER BOWL SUPERSTAR

Tight end Travis Kelce caught the football. He ran down the field to gain 22 yards.

Travis led his team with 93 total yards in the game. He helped the Kansas City Chiefs win the 2024 Super Bowl!

Travis was born in
Westlake, Ohio, in 1989.

Travis and his older brother, Jason, loved to play sports together.

They played on the same
high school football team.
Travis played quarterback.

After high school, Travis and Jason played football at the University of Cincinnati.

Travis became a tight end at Cincinnati. He played there for three seasons.

In 2013, Travis entered the NFL.
He joined the Chiefs.

Travis hurt his knee in his first season. He played only one game.

He worked hard to get better.

In both 2014 and 2015, Travis scored five touchdowns.

The next season, he gained more than 1,000 yards.

Quarterback Patrick Mahomes joined the Chiefs in 2017.

Travis and Patrick led the Chiefs to the 2020 Super Bowl. They beat the San Francisco 49ers.

In 2023, the Chiefs topped the Philadelphia Eagles in the Super Bowl. In the 2024 Super Bowl, the Chiefs beat the 49ers.

The Chiefs reached the Super Bowl again in 2025. This time they lost to the Eagles.

Travis is an NFL star. Some fans say he is the best tight end ever.

Travis will work hard to reach the big game again. Chiefs fans are cheering him on!

TRAVIS KELCE

CAREER STATS

GAMES PLAYED: 175

TOUCHDOWNS: 79

TOTAL YARDS: 12,166

SUPER BOWL WINS: 3

TRAVIS KELCE

GEAR

GLOSSARY

NFL: National Football League

quarterback: a football player who throws passes

Super Bowl: the NFL's championship

tight end: a football player who blocks and catches passes

LEARN MORE

Alinas, Marv. *The Kansas City Chiefs*. The Child's World, 2025.

Flynn, Brendan. *The History of Football*. Jump!, 2025.

Leed, Percy. *Football's Super Bowl*. Lerner Publications, 2025.

INDEX

PHOTO ACKNOWLEDGMENTS

Image credits: David Gray/Kansas City Chiefs via AP, p. 5; Paavo Turtiainen/Alamy, p. 6; Andy Lyons/Getty Images, p. 9; Stacy Revere/Getty Images, p. 11; Scott A. Miller via ZUMA Wire/Alamy, p. 12; AP Photo/Reed Hoffmann, p. 14; Scott Boehm via AP, p. 17; Michael Owens/Getty Images, p. 18; David Eulitt/Getty Images, p. 21; Cooper Neill/Getty Images, p. 23. Design element: liangpv/Getty Images. Cover: AP Photo/Steve Luciano.